Yusef Bushara

Good News

Yusef Bushara is a Sudanese-Bermudian writer, born and raised in Warwick, Bermuda. He has lived in Canada, France, Hong Kong, and is currently based in London. This is his first poetry collection.

The right of Yusef Bushara to be identified as the author
of this work has been asserted in accordance with
the Copyright, Designs and Patents Act 1988.

Copyright © 2025 by Yusef B. Bushara

All rights reserved. No part of this book may be reproduced
or used in any manner without written permission of the
copyright owner except for the use of quotations in a book
review. For more information, address: ysbushara@gmail.com

First paperback edition June 2025

Book design by Kayley Gibbons
Photographs by Nicola Muirhead, Jayde Gibbons,
Kayode George, Flora Chen and Yusef Bushara

ISBN (paperback): 978-1-0369-2160-6

Edited by: Sion A. Symonds
Typeset by: Kayley Gibbons

https://yusef-bushara.vercel.app/

The author thanks the Bermuda Arts Council for
the financial support of this collection.

beloved 8

Final Act 10

Emily 11

Dancing Feet 12

Pink 13

Limestone Languish 15

Bamboo and Skyscrapers 18

What's a Fresco Anyway? 20

Portrait of Mind at Riddell's Bay 22

See It 46

The Sandwich Man 48

The Dock 49

The Lane 50

Spithead Summers 51

God, What is Serendipity? 54

Hail to Bermudas 55

To Porto 56

In Praise of Your Fourth Dimension 58

I Had to Say 60

- Whataboutism 61
- Coastal People 63
- Cocooned 65
- Babies and Moths Born at Night 66
- "Animal House" 67
- I Couldn't Find the Duck When I Looked 68
- Mrs. Muir 69
- Refuge at Meroë 70
- Sands From Sudan 72
- 'Nuff Trains 74
- Hoodvogue 76
- Thank you, Grandad 77
- At a Loss 79
- november 80
- Who Do We Become by the Shadows Doing? 81
- Love in the Eye of a Storm 82
- Easier to Say the Easy Things 83
- acknowledgments 84

For Granny and يُمَه
in the hopes to make you turn our way

beloved

n. the sound of which being called,
necessarily by an aged soul,
makes one feel the deep satisfaction of
being caught on tenderhooks unexpectedly.

n2. a remedy that diverts the greyest day away from despair.

A Bermudianism; an imperative. False etymology: From *be*, natural state of existing
+ *loved*, saturated with light.
Pronounced "bee-luv-ed"; read "be-loved."

Final Act

I wonder if good words really
slide from the brain straight to the heart
I wonder if the spirit intervenes
when a poem is delivered home

I wonder about the great poets
like maya and mary
I wonder about the poems
they silently composed as their final act

I wonder what they left
for us to say to each other,
I wonder what they left
for us to find in awe

I wonder which of my words
belong to mary
and which to maya
and I wonder which of my words
belong to you

I wonder about the mountain
you read to me
and I wonder about the mountains
that sit atop your brain

I wonder how much cold and silence
it takes to agitate snow
I wonder how much snow
an avalanche needs
to slide the good words

straight from your brain
into your heart.

Emily

In the summer of 1993
Emily swept a small island
in the North Atlantic off its feet

The last blow of August
took us by storm and, though
I wasn't alive to remember her,
the chance at a summer romance is
still enough to make anyone pray to
a vague god or to a god vaguely
with clenched eyes and upturned palms

When Emily made landfall,
the number one song was
"Falling in Love with You" by UB40

The last blow of August blew as a kiss,
oh, that summer fling

Dancing Feet

We stole away from the rest of the group on our bikes in search of privacy / 70, 80, 90 meters ahead, however far away our legs would carry us before the remaining three recovered the gap we'd been working on all afternoon / Our adventure was drawing its curtains, and I wanted nothing more than for my feet to be still / We veered toward a fence on your whim and *it was beauty, I learned, that we risked our stillness for* / Nervous to live with abandon at 17, 18, 19 / Living freely is a recent inheritance I'm grateful for / I was in tow while our bikes stood watch / Dusk allured you to centerfield / You wafted ecstasy on your way to that center; you told me it was sweat / I told you / You were love—and we walked as one to the Douglas Fir ahead of us / You suspended your legs piggy-back-style and managed to kick in stride despite my bum hip / My eyes were forward when I felt our smiles sync / At the edge of laughter but not all the way there / My better senses buckled our rhythm, and soon my legs, when a gang of sheep challenged us to dance / I stuttered my two left feet into motion / I remember / I avoided the tops of your toes like surgery, all careful / We two-stepped as a four, let our shadows partake in their own romance / The herd didn't take heed of the signs, threatened what we'd created of that moment with a barely legible shuffle / Sheepish / My eyes over your shoulder couldn't hold them still / I stopped trying, stopped wandering, and returned my gaze back to you / Dreamy, North Atlantic Blue, with Saturn's rings wrapped around your pupils—where I recognized myself disbelieving that any of this could be real / We were happy and outnumbered by the spectacle of sheep on this farm ceding itself to evening / We were all spectacle to each other / You to me / Them to us / Nothing real / And all fleeting / The leader boasted black wool / He led the final number / Two-step / Two-step / Two-steps closer / The dancing sheep weren't dancing / It was our turn to move again / We mimicked the sheep: Two-step / Two-step / Two steps / We outran this fiction back to our bikes / We left our shadows at the center / On the way back, you paused me midway / Loosened me up like a thief, stole my rhythm and a kiss

//

Pink

I tell myself one lie whenever I slip into the water for a swim. I lie for my survival. Not sincerely but I chalk it up that way. I love the sea. Mostly how the surface complements the shades of pastel around the island, and the white roofs. The colors are more vibrant from the water. Any signs of an aging landscape are obscured by distance and the squint in my eyes when the sun's overhead. Same goes for Bermudians. Everyone is more handsome and younger when they tread water, but I've noticed I can't do it well. And it's a horribly sad thing. I wear glasses that aren't so thick but precious enough to my sight, that I take them off while swimming. The pastels dotting the landscape suffer from my shortsightedness while I'm out there, drifting. I bob just above the surface, and when I had a baldie, before my locs, from far enough away, I looked like a seal stranded. Like a seal mid-mice, ever so slightly satisfied that he's found himself in warm waters.

Though I can't see well, I know how the landscape figures. Its contours and colors. I've seen enough watercolor paintings in gift shops, and haven't always had bad vision. Plenty people hard of seeing love living by the water. I live by a busy road, which happens to be the island's main artery, and a golf course. The course is a green space teeming with incredibly small life and hibiscus: all the colors of swizzle, and sometimes pink. Golfers take no notice of these things. They stand there on the other side of the shrub. The one separating our house from the fourteenth tee. They stand arranged in a half-circle watching each other perform ritual movements. Chanting and then silent. Always a variation of the same motion, punctuated by colorful language distracting from the green around them. I don't live by the sea, but my vision makes it so that I listen for it well. As a writer, I prefer my awfully small ears. Always in the range of three to four seconds before I hear the ball meet the water. Not more than three to four seconds can a golf ball travel before meeting the sea anywhere on this island. And if I haven't heard a faint splash after five, I know the ball is safely on the fairway or salvageable in bushes further along. It never gets to six seconds of silence, there's too many roosters around at noon and tree frogs at dusk. Five seconds of silence is all the golfers can bargain for after making good on their backswing and completing their stick dance. The others bang on their chest. They are nomads, these golfers, notorious for their dislike of the water.

I walk to it—not to find golf balls—in the evenings, when the sunset is the color of the hibiscus, the color of swizzle. My eldest sister told me the best sunsets were predictable, that they'd leave hints in the day's cloud cover. Thick and porous sheets, slices of swiss cheese overlaid on a canvas I thought was universal until I went to places with buildings too tall for our kind of white roofs. Wispy clouds meant unremarkable sunsets, hardly a science. She was right no fewer times than I walked to the pink ferry stop to find an even pinker sunset making acquaintance with the birds, the beaches, the boats, the buoys, the boys, and all shades of black skin. I enjoy that synchronicity, when the colors above conduct hues on the things below.

There's a local celebrity. He drives a pink taxi. He wears pink socks pulled up to his knees. Pretend his knees are pink too for the consistency of this image. Let your eyes gaze up from the pennies shining in his loafers. He has pink shorts. An eight-inch inseam. Cool senior raised in, he'd tell you, more sensible times. Odds are, he wears something conspicuous and gold on his person and speaks with the warmest Bermudian accent while saying "Evenin." He sports a pink shirt and right above it a crystal smile. There it is, the piece of gold I was telling you about. Makes his crystal smile pierce. I wonder how he feels on hibiscus nights. Must be like God.

Sunsets aside, I still haven't told you my lie. But we're at the water now. I'm about to slip in and frig up the calmness of the surface. Beneath I know there are secrets I can't bear to swim with. I scream *hallelujah* in the name of pink Jesus; I tell myself the lie. My toes are flexed and my small ears sharp. I have a serious buoyancy issue flaring up. I sink as my ears fill. I fearfully listen out for the murmurs I think fish make. I forget that they don't care about the color pink and bad vision and my lying their existence away.

//

Limestone Languish

Our lyric has a sargasso timbre,
tepid and slimy tongues like quicklime ina bit of water
letters peel off quick and hot,
far from the speech of the man who greeted me
in the tone of *waddam* by his cliffs on Northshore.

With what attention his left eye could pay
his right was no better, looking at me neither,
looking up, he told me in jest that recent inflation
had even gotten his vision

He spent thirty years watching rocks
fall into the shape of porous souvenirs.

He held the remnants
until posterity pried his fingers open,
immortalizing his memory in those who stopped
those like me, who had time
and enough gratitude to repay
the attention his micing eye could not.

His flame endured for those cliffs
and the way they'd rubble,
wrinkling the water below
with the immensity of all they had lived to see.

"If this limestone could talk," he started,
sucking his teeth, silencing the next thought:
"I wouldn't have to be consoled
 by their falling apart."

For thirty years he stood beside them,
poet enough to summon story
from calcium carbonate crumbs
that never worshiped him back,

He confessed:

> I'm much the same
> as these rocks, dun
>
> I erode as they do—
> > hardly gently
> > > never all at once
>
> I'm an aquifer too
> with water percolating
> from beneath my surface
>
> Yet I'm cement-strong,
> like Rocky Bay stone, bie
>
> It's my flame
> burning beneath the kiln
>
> I give you my last
> story with the ferocity and languish
> of a Casuarina during The Tempest

Bamboo and Skyscrapers

In case I ever forget, I want something to show for how I tried to make a big place feel small. Vignettes with tea cake dimensions – all short and sweet – to tell my versions of the unseen life where smallness indulges detail. To be a god of small things. I go to the roof in my residence to watch small things shrink, the men assembling bamboo scaffolding across the street and how they become figurines. It is the first roof in my life whose danger doesn't unsettle me. To be high up and sure feels like the godliness of going to church after a hiatus spent without repent. I have thought about the worst on the roof; if one day my curiosity, more eager than my faith, makes me spill at the edge. I have been haunted by the image of falling so swift, breaking another pair of glasses, and going splat. The great equalizer is how we all splat in shades of red. I imagine those seconds like honey passing through a tube sock, the sticky thought of regret killing me first. Have I given myself a frivolous departure because I peered my head over an edge? Thought with a bit too much force? *Was it you, tiny human, who threw that egg at me in my dream last night?* That stuff happens, ill-inspired, ridiculous exits. This can't be tragedy, too. There's not been any struggle in that suffering. Upon my descent, I just know I'd replay the crunchy eggshell noises from my dream, a cruel taunt. Not noises but sounds. I'd imagine the eggshells laughing out their yolk guts, watching my fate unfold. We'd both just be a couple of humored, cracked bastards by the end of the ordeal.

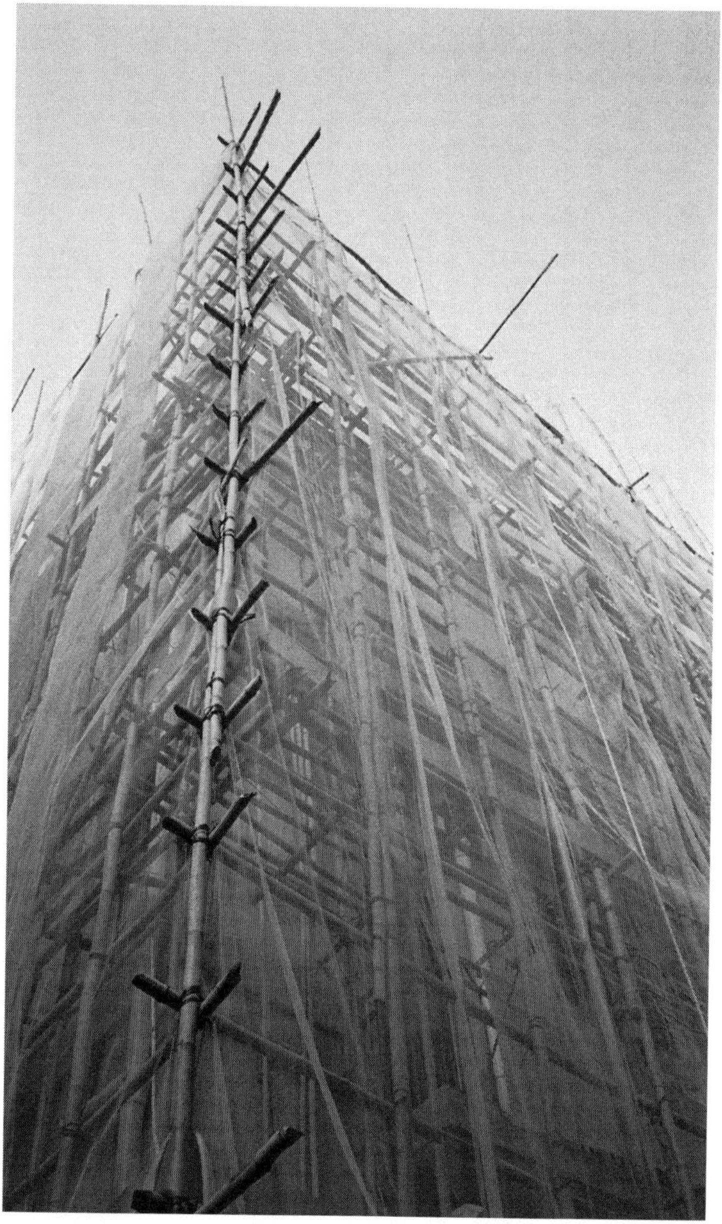

What's a Fresco Anyway?

I like the deep rouge
that drips out when
we prick our fingers while
stitching and unstitching traditions

I like the loose spots too
the spots we don't know
will one day give out

I like a tapestry that tears
and the thought of coming back
like a time traveling tailor
to touch up memories we share
with permissible lies

I like that we'll unravel and
always once more come together

How beautifying for the soul
this edifying tapestry

I like the thought of laboring
with you in the early morning
when things are made hard by
the salt of a day yet begun

Ask Michelangelo about
the Sistine Chapel,
if it was a mild matter
that he had nothing left
after wringing out his soul,
if an emptied soul is why
Adam's fingers even come
close to touching God's

Ask Him about luck and divinity
about how opposites attract
about how opposites made it possible
for him to bear an eternity spent
staring at a vanishing ceiling

Like the painter
I know what great deal I owe luck
because love
like art
is something surely divine
beyond the choice
of laboring hearts alone

//

Portrait of Mind at Riddell's Bay

I

I heard yesterday that the engine of a formula
one car can get to be half as hot as the surface
of the sun, a staggering twenty-six-hundred
degrees celsius. I can't imagine driving with
half the sun underneath my seat. I don't know
if I revere the sun as much anymore, now
that I know what I know. That it's just a little
hotter than a fast car. Lousy poster child of
heat. I think we should all revise our praise
for the sun, worship something that doesn't
claim to be supreme. Call a spade a spade:
say that the ball of fire works no harder than
two hot engines. In the sun's defense, I didn't
wake up today to watch an engine rise.

II

This morning is many perfect things, even in
the unpleasant sensations. I tolerate the long
grass tickling behind my knees. A kayaker
just came cross the sound moving fast. A dot
on my landscape. I'm thinking of that one
line in that poem – how does it go again –
so far from tribe and fire. Yes, the kayaker
made their way to the middle of the sound,
so far from tribe and fire. In the middle of a
sleeping blue crater. They didn't jeopardize
my solitude. Far enough away for me to
believe that neither of us existed completely
to the other. Far enough away to erase the
obligation I owe to a stranger: to consider
them as more than an object of poetic living.

III

There's a few more things I'd like erased
for this morning to be perfect. Get rid of
all the boats with an engine. The sailboats
can stay, though only if they're far enough
away to elicit the poetics of this landscape.
Any closer and the obligation returns.

IV

Get rid of the flies, goodness, and the cars. They cause me the same annoyance. I only know it as paranoia, the endlessness of an unease. I've never been enchanted by a fly or a car, never once caught their fleeting magic, and that alone makes me suspicious of their role here in my status quo.

V

Get rid of the houses.
 Leave the terrain green, unblemished, sprawling.
  Turn the island back to rock and forest,
   back to Venturilla's devilish expanse.
    Turn it back over to mystery.

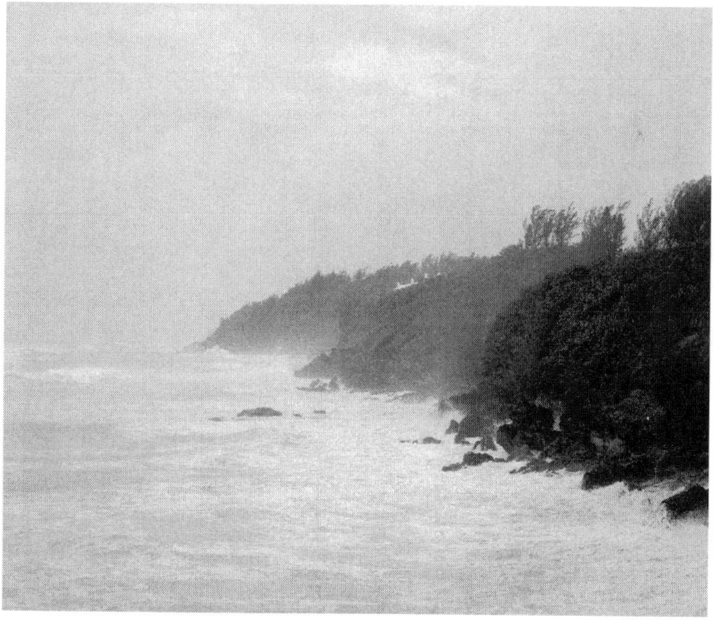

VI

Keep the bridges. Keep the mowed grass. Keep
the man-made docks. The Queen's bottom.
Just keep them empty. Keep the roads, only
cover them with tightly packed dirt. Make
the road a trail, bring back the railway. Keep
the train running this time, slowly. Guide
it quietly into the arteries of this land.

VII

The sun is up.

Can no longer flirt with the possibility of suspending the sky in pink, orange, red, yellow. I fell into a light sleep for about twenty minutes with my eyes. My brain took me to this stanza written by a poet selling individual poems in a park with yellow flowers. If artists must sell art to survive, may roaming in your favorite park be the model.

> *I wonder if birds*
> *are very light fish*
> *that live in the deep blue sky*

VIII

We'll keep the kiskadees too.

This is my vatic state. I keep telling people
I'm searching for delight. I don't know what
I'm searching for until I find it. I don't know
what I'm writing until I write it. This is my
vatic state. The hours do not move until I draw
my attention away from time. It's not easy
subjecting myself to boredom for the sake of
delight. I sit, I wait. The entire purpose of this
experiment is to see if I can make it to the end. I
told myself I was coming here to write a portrait
of my surroundings. Is this a self-portrait?

IX

There's a rock sticking its head out of the water that looks like a seal. First guess would've been that it was a seal, but I remember my marine science teacher telling us that seals only enjoy waters colder than these. She was an angel disguised as a teacher, habitually dressed in a bright yellow raincoat. I lived in a place called Pedder Bay, a divot on Vancouver Island's southern coast, home to an RV camping site, a teahouse with delicious cranberry scones, seals and sheep, and a small cohort of self-proclaimed changemakers who, on any given day, could be found among the sheep and the seals, doing unbecoming things above ground and on the sea. All of us lived together in this Great North American rainforest, and sometimes I thought Laura's raincoat, bless her, was the only derivative of sunshine I'd see until the spring. Then she'd smile amid raindrops on an autumn day. A friend told me yesterday that the water was twenty-seven degrees. Everything bless. The seals I learned about wouldn't survive long in bath conditions, the same way I couldn't survive long in cold water. I tried. Enjoying cold water is just one trait I don't share with seals. I can't swim very well either. I also can't hide that fact well.

X

The tide lowered. Where does the extra water go? I didn't learn that in marine science. The rock in front of me is no longer a rock on its own, there's now a bridge—something leftover from the volcano, I suppose—connecting it to the rest of the land. I wonder if lava gets only half as hot as the sun. Maybe it's the hot stuff beneath the earth's surface calling for our adoration.

XI

I grabbed tea with a favorite teacher the day
before yesterday. He took a medium coffee,
black as volcanic rock. We were at Rock Island
Cafe. We talked about bellhooks and black
girlhood; we talked about grief. He told me that
when his mother passed, he felt the absence of
her prayers. She was not a religious woman. He
felt the absence of her prayers. She was not a
religious woman, but he felt the veil drop. Made
me think about who's been saving me til now.

XII

Herons must be evening birds. I've seen about
six different types of birds this morning,
none of them herons. I am in Heron Bay.
There are only about six bird varieties in
Bermuda. But everyone and everything in
its time. *Take time.* They used to call this
underwater volcano Devil's Isle. Back when
they weren't familiar with birdsong. Now
the few cahows remaining are too scared to
leave their nest. Where are you, herons?

XIII

I heard someone sneeze but couldn't find
anyone to bless. Is it faith still when I whisper
'bless you?' Developers have steadily been
building mansions across this park, the
whole island really, the wealthy like moles
disappearing into their aboveground tunnels,
afraid of what I might say to their faces.

XIV

My dad was on the phone to his youngest sister
yesterday for an hour. She's the youngest sister
but all the girls were born first. Six of them,
and then the three boys, Amir, Bushara, and
baby Othmane. My dad is the second youngest.
Heir to no throne, if these were throne times,
which they still are in some places, like in
the place he was raised. A small island in its
own right. Which reminds me that I'd like the
Union Jack scrubbed off the Bermuda flag.
Just that. We'll keep the lion and the sailboat.

XV

I pray our island never knows the ugly faces of
war, however the thought of revolutionaries
hiding out in the mangroves satisfies the
corner of my imagination where freedom
resides. There's a distinct displeasure
I find in being a member of a colony.
Nobody else seems to mind. And you?

XVI

I understand that the revolution will
first be launched with love.

> *Good morning. How's your peoples?*
> *Would you like to go for a walk?*
> *Take these loquats.*
> *Longtails are my favorite summer bird too.*

XVII

My dad and aunt were speaking in Arabic.
The language that used to have the sole claim
to his thoughts. Before English required some
space. When I asked him what they were
talking about he told me he'd been having
trouble sleeping, was asking for advice.
Auntie Mona told him to buy magnesium.
You spoke about magnesium for an hour? I
didn't believe it, but I had no reason not to.

XVIII

In the language my aunt and dad spoke on the phone my last name, Bushara, means *good news*. Imagine we could choose our last names instead of being bound by their fates. That's not a world I want to write in.

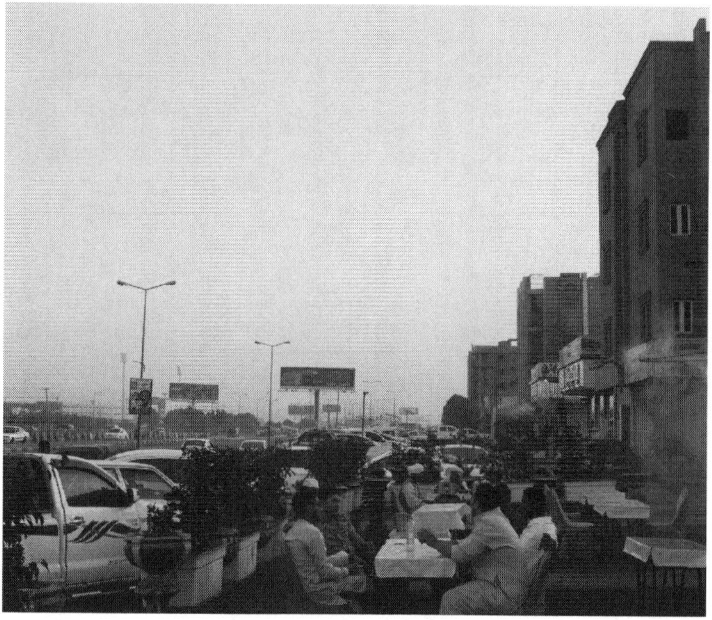

XIX

Above all else, I love it when a Stevie Wonder lyric
greets me in my silence and breaks it joyfully.
    Who will I call to say: I love you.

XX

There is a shadow of my hand
on the opposite page of my journal.
I couldn't explain to you
how that works with any kind of authority,
I don't care to,
I can try,
I'm drawing blanks
and my thoughts are drifting toward sundials.
Who are we
if not punctual
for the darkness that comes with all light?

XXI

Dogs sweat through glands on their tongues,
I didn't know this. They don't hide their
fatigue. They don't find it commendable to
keep their tongues in their mouth. They show
their sweat and plead for water, saying, *I want
to keep going, I've been honest about my thirst.*

XXII

A man with a hat on just told me to move from my spot on the grass. He surprised me. I asked him why I should move. All he could say was private, private, private. He had a small dog that looked like him and a voice I didn't much like. I all at once became conscious of my blood, felt its temperature rise and warm the surface of my skin. The man went silent amidst that momentary vacuum, and sensing my non-compliance, he became indignant—this stranger—turned indigo, his reddish skin mixing with the vacancy of my castigated, blued soul as he threatened to call the police. I don't know why people enjoy power in this way. I pushed my hair out of my face to see what kind of hat he was wearing, how wide its brim. At which point my voice started to tremble. I didn't want to move, I couldn't move. I was duty-bound. I was waiting for the herons to land and for the tides to rise again. Who else was going to do this job? He wanted the landscape for himself, the engined boats and the ones with sails; the birds, the silence, he wanted all of my fear for his own. I left. I put up my small act of resistance and called him a bastard under my breath. I was an object, obstructing his view. The difference between our solitudes were the lengths we'd go to for them. I didn't like his hat but I didn't think the feds were necessary for his indiscretion. We were in a park after all. I woke up early this morning and placed my beach chair on the hill. I wonder if it was him who sneezed? If he got my blessing?

See It

*Have sirens ever entered
the silence of your dreams?
Who does the noise conjure up?*

Have you ever seen us pop wheelies uphill / oblivious to ridicule and wide open / Have we ever delivered you a package / painted your roof / checked your meter / changed your tires / built your shutters / caught you a fish and then fileted you a fish / Have we ever told you good morning before you've really been awake / or goodnight long after you've checked out / Have we ever pumped your gas and wiped your windows so clear you wondered where we got our smile / Have you ever seen joy like ours as we read our books next to you / do our crosswords / talk our packs / Have you ever thought you was the first one out after a wicked storm and seen us restoring the lines in your hood / Have you ever spoken to us without finesse and been endeared by ours / Have you ever been surprised by this exaggerated swagger and tried it on / be honest / Have you seen how we sweet talk your granny / Have we said your granny could be your mother / given her a side squeeze that turns into a full squeeze / Have you seen us hug each other in tank rain / create the kind of electricity that don't flicker in storms / Have you seen our bodies slide like that on wet roads where bikes are sprawled / laughing road rash better / Have you seen us laugh with every part of our body except mouth / Have you seen us write poems / preach sermons / run real fast before sunsets on a Sunday / Have you heard us describe the sun indelibly / say things about it that it don't know about itself / Have you seen us takeoff from cliffs / Have you thought we could fly / until we crash / until we are shot out the sky / Do you see us / Will you see us?

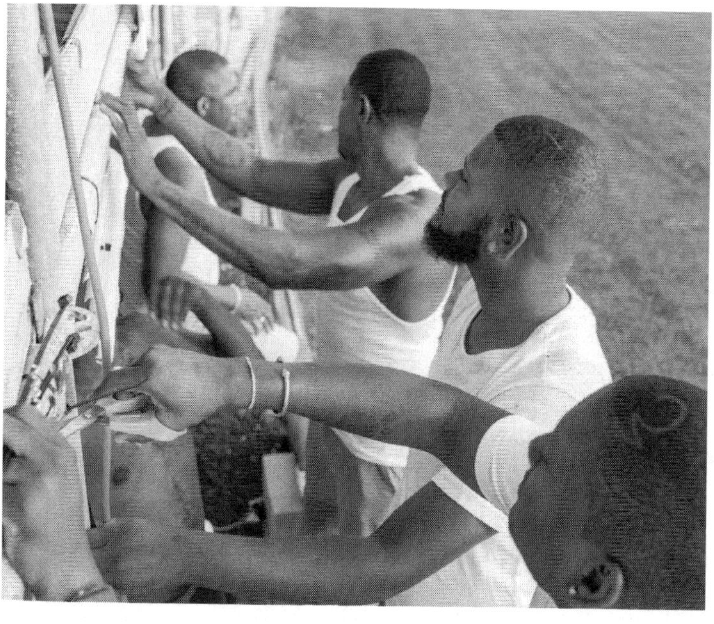

The Sandwich Man

The Sandwich Man
taught me about delight
during his lunch break

"Delight is grateful your ears
n eyes outnumber your mouth,
that you ought to use my beak
less than a feckless bird"

The Sandwich Man asked me
if I was hard of hearing
if I could I hear the
flightless sahn of cluckin n
kisskadees kissin teef

The Sandwich Man didn't want an answer,
just for me to close my beak and watch theirs work

//

The Dock

Imagine dangling feet at a dock
Imagine two sets of them
Imagine these four dangling feet
in conversation

Imagine one set leaves and
the other set stops dangling,
stops conversing

Imagine ya bredrin running and
sending it off the dock
Imagine the other set of feet
starting to dangle again, talking alone

The Lane

Consider the curious case of
lane names on this island

Consider the candidness of
Suffering and Pain Lane
East and West

Consider the playfulness of
Slippery Hill and Bat 'n Ball
if you will

Consider the searching mind
who ran out of time and
came up with Sofar, Narrow,
and No Name Lane

Consider our flora and fauna
making an appearance in
black n white

Consider all the fruits
Banana, Lemon Grove, Strawberry and
Peach Tree

Consider Kiskadee Drive and Hogfish Hill,
The Beehive
The Bluebird
The Herons Nest

Consider how obvious the choice
Christ, the steep one
to be
Up and Down Lane

Spithead Summers

I envy the force with which the sun turns my skin from brown to gold. I was sitting at the dock. "What's up, young blood?" A man made the jump from the small boat with an outboard engine to where I sat, nobody had time to tie up. He was holding a garbage bag which is only memorable because it didn't smell of anything. At Spithead, what you see and hear takes precedence. That's most places in Bermuda where the water is clear through to the bottom. That only leaves out the marshes and ponds. The two men who drove the boat to the dock where the jumping man got off, disappeared far along into the beam of light that made the water dance and my forehead drip. My eyes tracked a striped fish and burned from two streams of sweat flooding my sight like beaches along the Dead Sea. A sergeant major marched through several pillars of light standing slanted in the depth of the water, from bedrock to surface, like a family of sunflowers. I don't like the look of a fish unless it's passing through a beam of light because then I'm not reminded of fish, only of the golden color that makes everything about our crystalline surfaces magic.

For whatever reason, black men don't enjoy aging. Uncle Denis reminded me of this as he came down the steps at the dock. We played the game every older black man loves to play. I indulged him with a wildly flattering low-ball of a guess and his demeanor lifted while he peeled his shirt off. He's my uncle-by-marriage, and this is Bermuda. You have to flatter the people you see on fate's accord with all sorts of pleasantries. You also have to know that your uncle won't ever bump into you at the dock without a story to tell, and you're lucky if it's one. These are the guarantees in a Spithead summer, that you'll see someone who will speak to you like they know you, young blood.

I said fifty-five and he smiled. He said seventy-five and I joined him, smiling. This game keeps its shock-value no matter how many times you play. Black men keep getting younger in old age; black women too, but black women are private enough to keep their secrets to youth heart-close. By the time I picked my jaw up and dusted it off, Uncle Denis was back in Trinidad, telling me stories about the Windies cricket team and how blatant it was to identify who the Trinidadians were. A mixed bunch of Dougla people who might as well have had the flag painted across their hybrid complexions. Denis was a

Dougla himself, his mother Venezuelan, his grandmother Indian, so you can imagine what shade of brown he was, almost golden; and he was disease-free, he wouldn't let me forget. I joked that he'd left the second helping of doubles on the table during childhood lunches and that's why his arteries were still open.

As the sun moved lower, more people arrived. Evening settled into my disposition. I knew there was a story in me about to exit, because everything started to feel serendipitous. Like we were all a part of some Caribbean skit, just missing refreshments. My former Tech teacher walked down the steps, a sparrow sat next to me, fish came to the surface, a food delivery man parked his bike on the sidewalk above us, and everyone joined the chorus of this very Bermudian event. We felt like characters in some slice-of-life film. He remembered my last name but strained the veins in his forehead to recall my first. "Bushara," he called out. I was fine to leave it there and continue the conversation, but Uncle Denis interjected and gave him information that widened his cheeks into an exasperated grin, "Yusef, that's right. Yusef Bushara. How's your mom?" Then the Russell's came down from off Cedar Hill. Spithead was always spoken about in parish lore up there when I was a child. It must be a rite of passage to spend time here once you have enough distance from your childhood to make sense of it: Sitting off and thinking, swimming and thinking, treading water and thinking. *Spithead*. One of the Russell ladies locked up real nice, barely splashed too. Went under the water like covers. She began doing somersaults. Something about her movements were childish and made her feel not young but free. Uncle Denis didn't seem young but free, and same for my Tech teacher, not young but free as he strapped his goggles around his forehead and told me he was looking for turtles. As we spoke, their faces turned from brown to gold – not young but free in the Spithead summer sun.

//

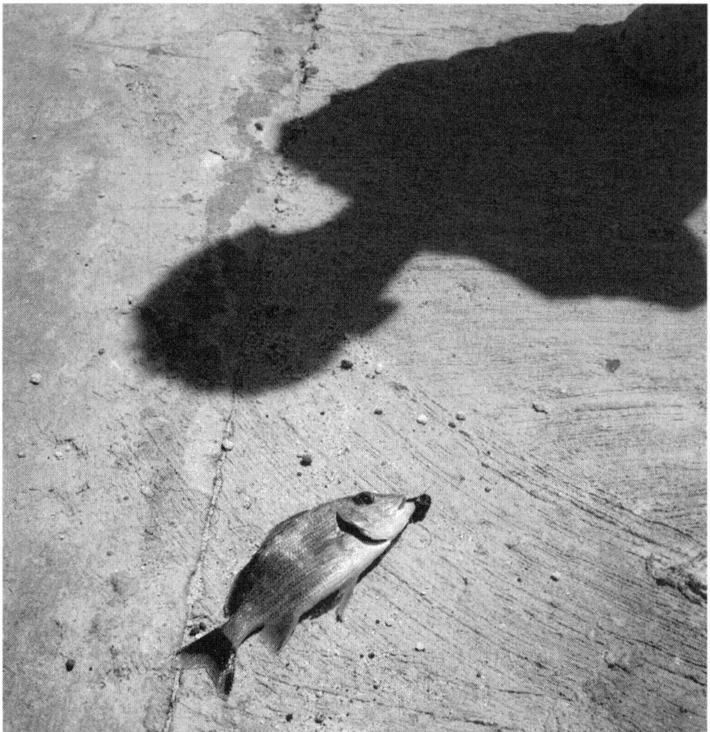

God, What is Serendipity?

God gave me a choice
by putting you
on my tongue's tip this morning,
and in front of me this evening

Believe in Him
or the serendipity
of a cove in a country as small

I asked God what that word meant,
before you slipped from my tongue,
becoming a memory whose name I'd never forget
not twice

Hail to Bermudas

Viva Bermudas,
Minhas ilhas ao sol.
Cante em glória
À nação em que nos tornámos.
Crescemos de coração em coração,
E de força em força,
É meu o privilégio
De cantar vida longa às Bermudas,
Pois estas ilhas são minhas!

Viva Bermudas,
Minha pátria benquista por mim.
Esta é minha terra
Construída em fé
E união.
Crescemos de coração em coração,
E de força em força,
Pois Lealdade é Primordial
Por isso, cante vida longa às Bermudas,
Pois estas ilhas são minhas!

To Porto

The sun has already gone packing for the day, the ball gone from
the sky. Some of the leftover daylight makes the clouds closer to the
river seem yellow while the rest are blue and cold like fall. There is
a breeze in the flat. I see a roof from my window and it looks like
the roof is touching the clouds. The roof isn't high so I wonder
if the clouds are feeling earthly tonight, low with the locals who
walk up these hills and still never reach high enough to grasp any
sense of the sky. I'm writing from a stranger's couch. I have a beer
opened on a stranger's table. The pleasantness of this vacation is
strange and unexpected. Natural then that I'm using a stranger's
things. If I poured my beer on to the blue clouds they'd turn a hue
of yellow similar to the ones hanging over by the river. I would do it
if I could reach the roof, soak the clouds with beer, but nevermind
the clouds and the roof. We can't forget who populates the sky. The
birds are here—somewhere. The ducks and seagulls; some pigeons
are making visits to shit on window sills, and the occasional parrot
is around, only the parrot is in my imagination and I've added
it to the scene for your sake of color, to draw out the feeling. For
such a vibrant city it has such ugly birds, this the deal it cuts for
its beauty. In Paris it is the people, no more flattering to speak to
than seagulls, and arguably just as stingy with their bread. There's
a clothesline I see from my window, too, with a red-and-white-
striped towel hanging from two pegs. I wonder who used it – what
for – whether used to clean a body or by a chubby Portuguese
child hiding the mess of spilled beer they weren't supposed to sip
from. The towel is tinted yellow the way cigarette fingertips can
be if the habit goes unchecked, whether from the light leaving the
surroundings or the beer, I don't know. The clouds are now pink
and orange, as pink as they are orange, a medley of warm tones
with colder undertones. Blue undertones. Ones brought to life
in a European city on the brink of a warmer season, I suppose,
like we are now. People during summer fall in love to skies like
this, turning slightly more pink. Don't our insides turn pink when
we love, our insides like a mass of all the world's bubble gum.

Don't we live to get chewed up, inflated until we think we won't burst, rounded in that glory, then to be spat out, with whatever's left of love stuck to our cheeks for someone else to taste. I saw a couple yesterday who must've broken up, though that sky was more orange than pink. In what colors does love leak? When people puncture love, burst the bubble, does it leak orange into the sky? Theirs was a stale feeling under a pretty sky, which frightened me. I don't want to feel an ounce of something on this vacation I might come to regret, even if that's a bad mood, not while the skies are like they are now, starting to look more red than pink. I'm mostly love but not quite spat out yet; I feel like the combination of colors that have turned my evening over. I'm mostly sweet, like pastel de nata made blindly with sugar by the chubby cherub's avó – and I am thinking of how awesome the color yellow can be with a little char – or charm. The light is going faster than I can write and the evening is turning blue. Next to the towel a pair of blue jeans hangs from two pegs and I'm wondering if they belong to the invisible woman whose shoes we saw by the river or if she, like me, is also watching the sky turn over to black here in Porto.

//

In Praise of Your Fourth Dimension

Some of the most beautiful things have three dimensions
like the human heart with its height, width, breadth
capable of love

Some of the most beautiful things are only wide
like long lines of poetry running for   margins
and running for them until the page is turned

Some of the most beautiful things have depth with no width
like the human soul, plenty deep
hardly fit for any page

The most beautiful thing is anchored by a fourth dimension
imagine the depth of the human soul twice over or two souls
with the reach of an unbound epic poem in gale force wind

The most beautiful thing cradles time and is
No less capable of love but
All the more willing to do it forever

The most beautiful thing is you, my brother
as the sun crowns your chipped tooth and
lights your jack-o-lantern self from the inside out

The most beautiful thing is your fourth,
It is time and how you make it feel to us
like it might keep its legs at the end of our story

//

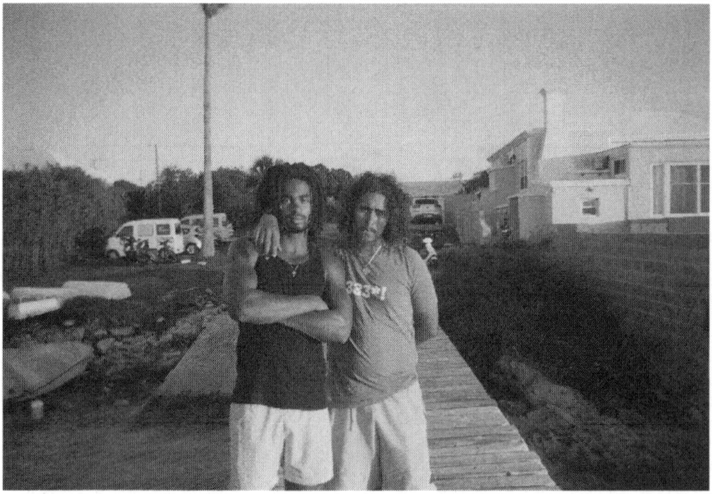

I Had to Say

I did not plan on bringing
you coconut water today
not on bringing you croissants then
for most things
I had just been laughing with a friend
on a train ride when
joy brought you to mind
we had no business laughing
creases into our faces, young
on such a quiet ride, old people
all around us, creases
without laughter
headed for a place called central
I dislocated my pulse
grew to like the uneven rhythm of joy

I mean we're just boys
we dance on trains
where nobody laughs
all with our shoulders
pretending to bossanova
our hips into a verb
The truth is this
I brought you two
miniature croissants
because I saw your eyes on the window
Two plums
One more than usual
William Carlos Williams
Oh yes *This is Just to Say*
Forgive me for bringing you
coconut water, so sweet and cold

Whataboutism

What about the two birds
sat on the railing
and the porcupine
messing through the foliage?

What about dew
is especially true?
What about the touch of light
that turns grass gold
and Rufus the dog?

What about the way he runs,
and his tongue?
What about a reservoir
cut into the close of a mountain's back?

What about divine surgery
at the 6am hour?
What about the lady
who can't help her smile?

What about her gold,
is gold?
What about these tufts of grass
reclaiming the pavement?

What about taking back?
What about a flower
or a cemetery
or a dirty mirror?

What about a shadow
cast on the other side
of a colosseum?
What about triumph?

What about a crush
 makes you valiant
 without losing?
 What about all seven wonders of the world
 and this feeling being another one?

What about the eighth wonder
 being quiet mornings,
 birdsong,
 and water
 in the belly of this mountain?

Coastal People

Coastal people don't always live by the sea. They frequent it, and when they do, they like to occupy their hands. A book, a cigarette – both – the hand of another. I don't smoke, so I choose the book or the hand. I don't mind having one in either palm. That weight balances me. The book should be beach-fit. Already tattered, yellow from the cigarette smoke of someone, and written by a never-heard-or-seen-before author. A careful ghost who bears a name. Now, the hand should feel comfortable while it rests in yours. You don't need to have known the person for long—names are still not required as trips to the coast can arouse peculiar instances of spontaneity. However, you should feel safety by their grip. Enough to reciprocate it when waves crash toward you. The golden rule. Squeeze hands when waves crash. Don't worry about the book getting wet.

The author of the book should be of no distraction to those who walk by you. The book is merely a buffer between you and that crashing sea you sit before. *Ocean* isn't a word in the lexicon of coastal people, but sea is abused. The sea is a literary place, much more than the coast, which is why coastal writers have appropriated its nature in their musings. The distinction between the sea and the coast is the line between. It is approaching imaginary, but at some point the sea becomes the coast. Wherever that line lives, however thin, that's where writers perch themselves. A step behind, that's where the rest of the coastal people reside. The writers think they have the best view of the sea because they're the closest. They think the salt spray makes their words have an edge. Usually, the sea erodes the truths they try to profess. The smart ones retreat into the ambiguity and hideaways of poetry. The smartest ones don't write at all; they sit above the perched writers, up on the tops of sand banks, nestled on cliff sides, or sat with their legs swinging from side to side on docks.

The sea isn't always in a rush to crash. The dock is where coastal people go when the sea refuses to be aroused by the moon. It's sacred. Worship there happens with the homely flick of a rod. Maybe fishing line bridges the coastal people to the sea, almost thin enough to be imaginary. But when it yanks, there's no denying that the line is there. Coastal people enjoy fishing to pair with their smoking, reading of ghosts, and holding hands. In the midst of these coastal rituals, their landlocked counterparts live differently tempered lives. *Truly landlocked people know they are,* such are the words of Toni Morrison, our beloved. The landlocked might even venture to call the sea ocean if they never see first-hand how inappropriate that word is to describe what's there underneath the swinging feet at the dock. I'd be troubled to trust the words of a coastal person describing their surroundings in a landlocked setting. But I'd smile at the eloquence of the coastal writer asking the landlocked one what they preferred to be called.

//

Cocooned

I once had a butterfly live in my stomach,
just one, with a misplaced sense of humor.
It took pride in its idiom, and could make me
terribly nervous with a series of maneuvers done
below my diaphragm. A sweet butterfly dance.
When someone would ask of my anxiety I'd tell
them of this butterfly dancing in my stomach.
I didn't think too much about how or
why it ended up there,
My stomach was the darkest place in the world that
would stay dark forever. If I missed the womb like the
butterfly missed its cocoon, maybe I'd swim
for the bottom of the ocean, too.
Or anywhere so solitary.

//

Babies and Moths Born at Night

who don't yet know
that life must be lived
as much in darkness
as in light
do you worship sputtering
street lamps like there's
no tomorrow
until tomorrow comes
and teaches you
the meaning of the sun

//

"Animal House"

Mom tells me
she almost died
twice now in
as many days

this just after
my sister pointed out
the high-horse
between my legs

my sister wrote a song
which reminds me of
her fondness for
animals living out
side of these insults

goes something like
i've got a frog
in my throat
and he wants
to lay down

it was then i prayed
metaphors

the gene for them
comes from mothers

I Couldn't Find the Duck When I Looked

There are nuts, bolts, and screws
in the stew when I ask,
yesterday, peas were in the pot
and a duck was around the corner
this is dinner at our home:
sisters and dad eat duck,
dad leaves the meat on the bone,
only takes the skin
and traps it under his fingernails
to show he's paid dinner a visit

When we eat nuts and bolts,
he likes hummus on the bolts,
while sisters prefer the bolts mostly dry,
on the side,
perhaps ketchup,
one of them always with a glass of juice
to wash out the metallic taste,
the other doesn't mind,
has milk from the carton

Dad's stories come to life
when he rubs his belly anticlockwise,
as if he controls time with that gesture,
yuma's pot had no bottom, he swore
she kept two ducks at bay
behind the corner with her eyes alone,
how he found that strange,
that they were ducks that clucked

I wanted to ask him a question
before he went upstairs,
if yuma put the nuts in the stew
before the screws
if your eldest sister liked juice
if you told mom how much you loved her,
for making a stew
when there was nothing?

Mrs. Muir

I can't love someone who doesn't return waves
nor can I love everyone
who doles them out like donuts
but broke, I'd find the dough
enough for a dirt cheap flail of my dainty arm

Mrs. Muir sells summer
squeeze and seamoss down on southshore
She once gave me her hand full of ice
because she believed what I started to say
that my friend is tragically anaemic

The faithfulness of fruitjuicesellers is second
only to the faithfulness of rain during flood
When Mrs. Muir put the ice on us
it was cool and brilliant
burned our fingers until they sang and just for a moment
at our coolest, most brilliant
frostbitten and baked in Bermudian sun, just then
as we made that mass melt, we turned Cinema on its head
sunk an iceberg into the ground

//

Refuge at Meroë

I am the shade beneath the camel's belly
I am down-to-earth unlike my creator
I am ice in an oasis like this one

> Drink me, though, and still thirst
> Don't mistake me for my
> more acrobatic cousin, the shadow
> He who thrives off imitation. No, I am Shade.

Time old as Amanitore is stored in my lazy, cool protection
Bargain for me underneath this hydrated creature
in this land of pyramids where sun is sand-cheap

//

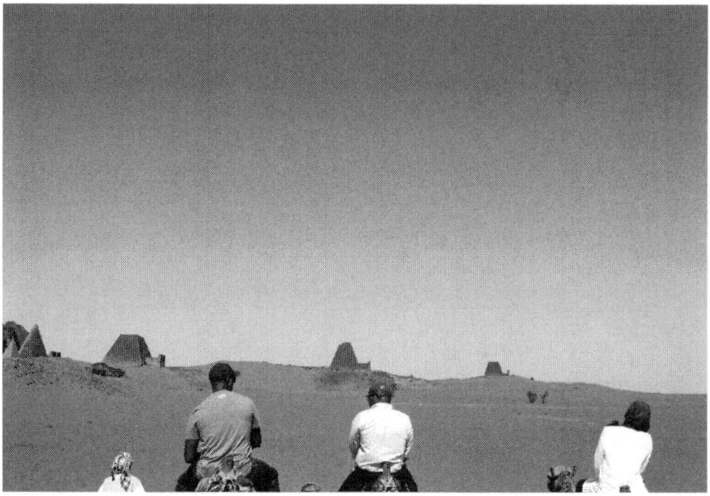

Sands From Sudan

I was told once that the wind carries sands from the Khartoum across The Continent to its coast, then from its coast and across the ocean. For a grain of sand, the desert is infinity and then the ocean infinity again. When you're in the air for as long as a grain of sand traveling twice across infinity, the novelty of flight wears off after about one thousand sunsets. Sometimes I think of all of the grains of sand in the sky on their odysseys, who have forgotten they belong to the desert. Another day, another infinity. I was brought up on pink sand, not the orange kind of my father's home. Sitting with my neck on the edge of the kitchen sink, I fought cramps while my mother scrubbed pink particles from my scalp after a day at the beach. Tender loving—she would tell me that for every pink grain she'd find, there'd also be an orange one. To distract my pain, she told me the story of the wind and how it carried sand from the Khartoum, twice across infinity, and directly to my scalp for her to scrub. She would stretch her storytelling and tell me of my father's father who, after playing outside with the same trifling abandon, tracked the desert back into his mother's house. My father teased me that no matter how hard I shook my head, there'd always be an equal amount of orange grains left behind, housed there between strands, for every pink grain my mother managed to rid my hair of. The orange grains of sand were from my father's desert, the pink ones from the beach, but the hair both were found in, came from my mother's mother. That was the wind's beauty, the way it carried sand into my grandmother's hair. She's met the desert through me. I'm reminded of this each time my mother pulls too fondly on the strands connected to my tender head.

As a child, I'd go to the beach and collect pink particles in my fingers. I'd hold them as tightly as my hair was coiled and, on a hurricane day, I'd take this pink pile of the unknown and release it to the swells, in the direction of infinity. I'd hope that one grain of sand would be steadfast enough to venture past its thousandth sunset. I wanted one grain of myself to make its way back to the desert without knowing it ever belonged anywhere else. Maybe somewhere in the sands of Sudan, lodged in the same dunes my grandfather trifled in, there's a pink particle without its memory.

//

'Nuff Trains

IIt was the last of seven trains I'd taken that day, all of them with Trenitalia except the first. I'd boarded that train in Menton, the first Italian city geographically in France when traveling west along the Ligurian coast. I was up at a sunless hour I'd avoid for the rest of my week off. Something to note before making a fatal seven-train attempt through Italy in one day, is that you'll likely not be where you intended to be at the time you intended to be there. Traveling a happy traveler is knowing that before boarding the first of those seven trains. Italy is filled with consolations for disaster, and even if you miss all but the first train, the one that, really, left from France, you'll end up in a quaint Italian place home to someone you met years ago, who lied for your sake and told you they were from a larger adjacent city. In this town/village/place, you'll end up on the train platform, no doubt visibly in disarray, wide-eyed and weary, watching, you've convinced yourself, the most breathtaking sunset to have graced the world that day.

I was lucky when I arrived in Verona in time for sunset; I was where I intended to be exactly when I intended to be there. Where I was going was further along the Adige, which you can imagine I pronounced wrong when I read it off the front of a newspaper the following morning in my destination place. It was a town with village undertones and village rhythms during colder months when tourists flocked for the larger adjacent cities. When I arrived in Verona, I was mostly desire. I considered staying because I'd read somewhere that love in that city could make you do foolish things. I wasn't about to tempt the worst of fate by sabotaging the good luck I'd fallen on. I was lucky that day, wide-eyed and staring directly at where the sun had been moments before, as my train prepared to pull out of the station.

This was on a night after I found out that the Adige was the name of the newspaper because it was also the name of the river in this town, the same one that ran through Verona. I hadn't kissed a stranger or done anything entirely plausible like that, but I was sat across from someone who knew exactly the gravity of my desire from a different time in our lives. I was eating strangolapreti in a cavern-turned-restaurant the evening after quiz night. I could tell there had been passion emptied out in this room recently, the floor sticking to my feet. The night before, beers were toppled and patrons were strangled by other patrons in spontaneous demonstrations of cathartic anguish. I imagined the strangling after my friend told me what "strangolapreti" meant. This cave's clientele seemed exactly the type to strangle the priest, whose side-hustle was to be a quizmaster, after answering incorrectly to the question: What is the second longest river in Italy? It was a northern take on gnocchi, made with stale bread instead. Nothing about the energy in this place was small potatoes. The last time catastrophe swept through it was wartime and the locals still found enough flour to create a consolation for disaster good enough to eat by the river.

//

Hoodvogue

Hoodvogue is from the cracks
like a hibiscus from limestone
flowers of life that stay stone-wedged, storytelling
wall-sitters are the prophets
testifying to life without soil
graffiti tributes are plastered scripture

Breaking news as quarry blocks fall
targets don't fade,
they shift and multiply,
the impossible becomes vacant on a once-white tee
and the scripture goes from the wall,

To your chest. Hoodvogue.

Thank you, Grandad

I bumped into a friend's grandad at lunchtime today in front of City Hall. It's the end of July. I knew it was lunchtime because there was a fairly large group of children together in a public area. The children themselves weren't large, I don't mean. Normal-sized if I had to say, but I don't know when I'd have to say. I had also set my parking meter at 11:55, and the walk to City Hall was three minutes plus two minutes, and I had to add the two minutes to account for the old faces I'd greet along the way. Such is Town and the whole island by foot. Between the children and the parking meter, I concluded it was lunchtime. There is also a clock plastered to the top of the City Hall facade, though I don't often look up in Bermuda unless to see a version of something that has always been there, like a star. Like the sun lowering itself from the sky and below the sea, as if being dangled slowly by a god like an old pocket watch. But never a clock. I have a watch that goes on my wrist. Tracks my heartbeat as well, tells me when to exhale – strangely. The children must have been part of a popular camp, such was their excitement, and the kind with a waitlist, such were their numbers. The kind where, no, not a few more, not a few more than a few more, no; the kind where no amount of money slipped into a registration envelope could help the fact that "No space remains for the following weeks." The kids were plenty, running in unpredictable patterns, like a swarm of drunken bees, making a composite drone of high-pitched sounds which, if stretched, could be called language. Or maybe some distant cousin of it. I love seeing which sounds make the cut. Which sounds creep beyond the threshold of noise to become intelligible, if not meaningful, if not hard-wrought, oil-stained, flat-out language. I love when a person understands my mumbling, or when I know exactly whether a car horn means thank you or thank you very, very much. The acoustics of any voice are delicious to me, the quality of sound laid completely bare. What a treat. We were sat in grandad's car for not more than a minute when one girl screamed, it seemed, because she suddenly remembered—and thus couldn't resist the urge to use—her voice. That she had a voice capable of inciting disturbance and play. Grandad is nearly 89 and often asks me to repeat things.

It's much better to deflect when speaking about the age of someone who's lived as long as grandad has. Yes, I could've said he's 88, but I want to take you directly to the fact that he's almost 89. Almost 90! Almost, as I see it, a century old. So, yes, granddad is almost 89 and with that comes the supernatural ability to block out much of the auditory world, including screaming children. We began our conversation with him in the car, me squatting awkwardly outside of his window with the kind of posture that would suggest that I had other things to do. I was uncomfortable not because I hadn't, within a few moments, resolved to stay; it's just that recently I've found out about the presence of a small lump in my groin, something called a hernia, which if I didn't know better, I'd think was the name for a concept in the realm of language. A favorite realm of mine, just after sleep. Sounds like a word given to the feeling of not being able to express oneself in the way one would like. I have a hernia. As a matter of fact, I have hernias all the time. I tried to tell grandad that I appreciated all of his stories so much, so deeply. I just couldn't make any of the words work. Forgive me for my small lump, grandad.

//

At a Loss

when there's nothing to say,
bare your heart
if you can't find it in yourself
to bleed, embrace silence
enjoy what may grow there
cover your quiet in algae and small
critters, decorate it nicely

november

november wastes no time unsettling brittle bones / or
brittle leaves on trees that shed grief in piles / not half as
low as the blues painting moonlit mornings / and glinting
afternoons spent paralyzed in untraceable lowness /
hostage to a breath that inhales me with daggers / in my
chest the fraughtness of silence is broken only by screaming
ink / a metaphor best kept for my parents who resent
tattoos because ink reminds them that november took
their parents and left their skin as memory / grief rests in
the hammocked wrinkles of their smiles / welds daggers
into life near the craters soothed eyes make / despite the
sharpness in our bellies / they've remembered me how
to hold a friend's hand in a november of loss / and how to
hold a friend's hand who doesn't know loss / or anything
else brittle and so forever as this month that stops the
clock to stow away time in my doing of all things / except
for my rest / stubborn daylight / alone / in november / i
surrender thanks for the helluvit / for gratitude's doors
to open on ease whenever she decides to enter again

//

Who Do We Become by the Shadows Doing?

Fragmented matter will scatter across skin
and open galactic wounds, and I mean stars, not wounds
There will come a day in each of our lives
when stars hold our bodies hostage
not unlike love in a breezeless summer vacuum
We will hold each other long, close, not know why
and we will understand that our skin
our ephemeral epidermis, is the container for withering light
We will hold each other questionlessly, fast and close
and our hearts will pulse in anticipation of dying stars
and the end the endless dawn of the shadows
I will hold you until that day when, tethered, we become a supernova
exploding all the matter that's drawn my body into yours

Love in the Eye of a Storm

This hurricane is an indecisive lover / Can't make up its mind whether to stay or leave / We're approaching hour twenty-four in an interminable catastrophe / I prefer the French pronounciation of that word / Three beats to our four / Time in a storm, like time during the summer, has a warped sense / Feels like taffy, stretched out and moist / Not at all brittle the way winter is, or peppy like spring / Clings to itself masturbatorily / Entertaining at the beginning, the howls and the ghouls / Twilight / Not knowing if seconds are moving by / Stagnant now / I'm tired now / Still / Feels like I'm covered in a rather heavy coat of mucus from my head and to the waterline just above my ankles / Sweat is the word / I don't know if you'd kiss me in this state / I've napped more times than I can count and in each of them I've willed my thoughts toward you / Those have been the only romantics during this storm / The dozen daydreams about us / There's been no running in the rain or getting struck by lightning in the name of some great potential / The only thing which could be misconstrued as romance is the amount of times I've called for love / Love, come here / Love, let's go for a short walk / Love, are you breathing okay? / Please don't hold it against me, that I call you by the name of Quincy's asthmatic Frenchie

Easier to Say the Easy Things

You don't have to say profound things now
Better you say the easy things
The obvious things, the ones in front of you

The birds are coming home
Summer is not the season for roses
You smell very, very sweet
Thank you for calling me beloved
My dad seems to have shrunken slightly
The sun set one minute earlier today

Say things out of order
and refuse to look back
Utter very forgettable mess
and roll on with the nonsense,
roll on with it

My dad is coming home
The roses smell very, very sweet
The birds called me, beloved
The sun seems to have shrunken slightly
Summer set one minute earlier today

Say the easy things now
and listen for the world's gratitude,
it will be a whisper
you giant pile of gorgeous wisdom

.

acknowledgments

This collection is a constellation of love, labor, and subtropical serendipity. It's with an enormously grateful heart that I offer these acknowledgements.

To Sudan, my distant home, land of Black poets and resistance—thank you for compelling me to write. I pray for an end to war, for a liberated Sudan where poets are no longer forced to document devastation, but are free to imagine and build what comes after.

To the home of my birth, Bermuda—there is no collection without a life shaped by your warmth. I am thankful for my parents, Anita and Bushara, and my sisters, Hana and Reem, for guiding me through the earliest days of that warmth and for showing me that there is light to be found in all places and small places. I thank my boys for their unwavering support, laughs, and encouragement: to you, Emad, Q, KJ, Hovie, Zach and Aditya, for always drawing me out of myself to experience joy and take life less seriously. I thank Nathaniel for being an incandescent force of love in my life and the inspiration for several of these poems. I thank Vaishali for your tenderness in the form of cups of chai, handfuls of nuts – and for having steadfast patience with me as I find my feet. I thank Toby and Quincy for the gift of decades-long friendship. I thank Justin and Jordan and Sion for the robustness of their faith in all things. I thank Lily for letting me love deeply and for loving me. I thank my dearest Flora, McKenzie, Amani, and Auntie Robin for showing me that it is always possible to give and to give and to be restored through that act.

A soulfelt thank you to everyone who's helped in the construction and editing of this collection. Thank you to Jordan Bolay for being the earliest eyes on my work six years ago, when this journey began in a forest on Vancouver Island. Thank you to Nicola and Jayde for testifying to the essence of life on the rock through your powerful photographic contributions, especially in your exhibitions *Descendants of Summer* and *My Negus for Real*, which are featured in this book. Thank you to Adrian for your kindredness, creativity, and always critical eye. Thank you to Kayley whose creative vision brought this book over the finish line. I'd like to thank *antilang, The Foundationalist, Underbelly Press,* and The *Caribbean Writer*, for showing earlier versions of "Dancing Feet," "Refuge at Meroë," "See It," and "Thank You, Grandad" to the world.

To the teachers of my life, Mr. Wade, Mr. Hammer, and Dr. Richards, thank you for teaching me the value in seeing small steps as still steps forward. To the many who have graciously held fragments of these poems throughout the years, thank you. And to all the writers without whom this work wouldn't exist: to James Baldwin, Mary Prince, Mary Oliver, Maya Angelou, Ocean Vuong, Toni Morrison, Jamaica Kincaid, Kamau Brathwaite, Yesha Townsend—thank you for being the literary giants of my life whose words on no few occasions have returned me home amidst fluctuating tides.

With warmth,
Yusef

Made in the USA
Columbia, SC
10 June 2025